Skin Like Milk, Hair of Silk

For Jimmy
—B.P.C.

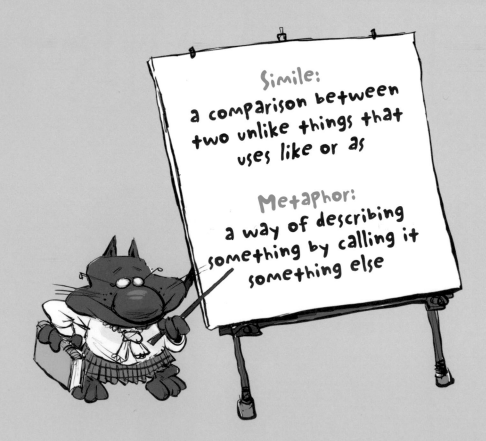

Simile:
a comparison between
two unlike things that
uses like or as

Metaphor:
a way of describing
something by calling it
something else

Skin Like milk,

Hair of Silk

What Are Similes and Metaphors?

by Brian P. Cleary

illustrations by Brian Gable

M MILLBROOK PRESS / MINNEAPOLIS

Similes are phrases that compare two unlike things.

As in, her hair is soft as silk.

Just like these,
all similes
contain an as or like.

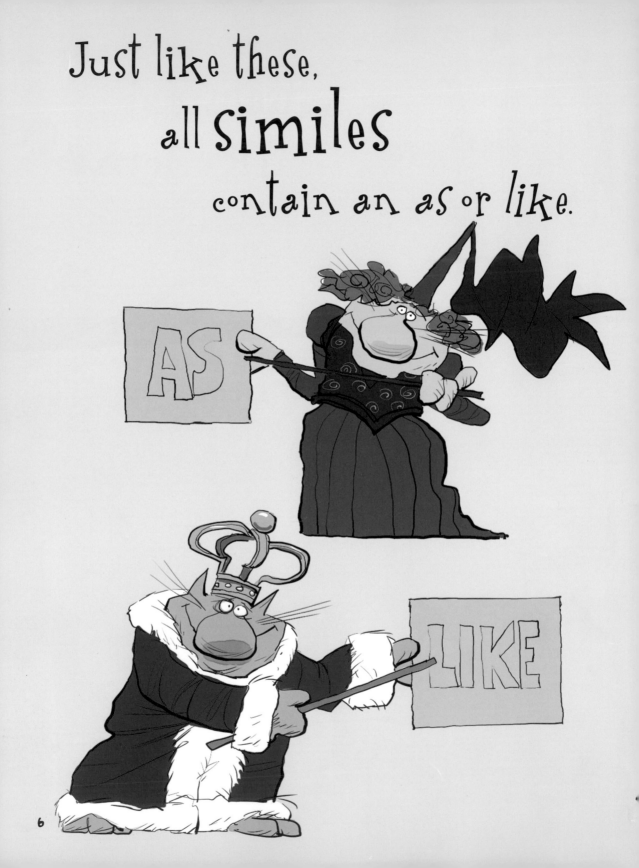

Smooth as jazz,

skin like milk,
and cheeks as red as roses.

8

Similes compare things,

like, "My dad's as old as Moses."

Similes can help you say that someone in your class is

as bright as polished pennies

They're helpful in describing people, things, and even places,

like,
fresh as
folded laundry

They help you paint a picture
you can see inside your brain—

like, he's clever
as a fox,

or her tears ran like rain.

Once you learn about them, they can change your writing habits.

You'll write one, two,

and then a few—

they'll multiply like rabbits!

As in, you are my sunshine.

or this singer is a star!

All of these are
metaphors,

just like,
his voice
is froggy.

Even chill out or be cool,

a heated conversation.

An icy glare, a frozen stare,

a very warm ovation.

At times, a sense of touch
is at the root of such a phrase:

a Velvet Voice,

Your work is sure to blossom

with similes and metaphors—

no doubt it will be awesome!

So what are **similes?**
What are **metaphors?**

LIKE

AS

Find activities, games, and more at
www.brianpcleary.com

ABOUT THE AUTHOR & ILLUSTRATOR

BRIAN P. CLEARY is the author of the best-selling Words Are CATegorical® series, the Math Is CATegorical® series, the Adventures in Memory™ series, and the Sounds Like Reading™ series. He is also the author of The Laugh Stand: Adventures in Humor, Peanut Butter and Jellyfishes: A Very Silly Alphabet Book, and two poetry books. He lives in Cleveland, Ohio.

BRIAN GABLE is the illustrator of several Words Are CATegorical® books, as well as the Math Is CATegorical® series. Mr. Gable also works as a political cartoonist for the Globe and Mail newspaper in Toronto, Canada, where he lives with his children.

Text copyright © 2009 by Brian P. Cleary
Illustrations copyright © 2009 by Lerner Publishing Group, Inc.

Millbrook Press
A division of Lerner Publishing Group, Inc.
241 First Avenue North
Minneapolis, MN 55401 U.S.A.

Website address: www.lernerbooks.com

Library of Congress Cataloging-in-Publication Data

Cleary, Brian P., 1959—
    Skin like milk, hair of silk : what are similes and metaphors? / by Brian P. Cleary ; illustrated by Brian Gable.
       p.   cm. — (Words are CATegorical)
    ISBN: 978-0-8225-9151-1 (lib. bdg. : alk. paper)
    1. Simile—Juvenile literature. 2. Metaphor—Juvenile literature. 3. Figures of speech—Juvenile literature. I. Gable, Brian, 1949— ill. II. Title.
PE1445.F5.C54 2009
808—dc22   2008049643

Manufactured in the United States of America
1 2 3 4 5 6 — JR — 14 13 12 11 10 09